Look What Rolled In

by Richard C. Lawrence
illustrated by Doug Roy

MODERN CURRICULUM PRESS
Pearson Learning Group

Long ago, there were no ball games. There were no balls to play with. There was not as much fun!

One creature looked up. It saw something. Then all the creatures looked. They all saw it.

Look what rolled in! It was new. It was round. Was it fun?

What was it?
The creatures didn't know.
How did it get there?
The creatures didn't know.
What was it for?
The creatures didn't know.

They looked at it.
It sat on the grass.
Was that supposed to be fun?

Then a new creature came.
"Do you like the ball I gave you?" he said. "Let's have fun with this ball!"

"You can throw it!
You can kick it!
You can catch it!"

"We have a big ball.
We have a little ball.
We have a round ball.
We have a not-so-round ball."

"We can play this way!"